AUTUMN'S

SONG

Inspirational Poems

ABSTRACT
Poems of inspiration dedicated to the growth of God's children. My hope is that the reader finds comfort and hope in their walk with Jesus on the straight and narrow path leading to heaven!

Daryl Williams
[Course title]

Autumn's Song

When Winter's passed

With stormy blast,

And calls up from the dead,

It's found so nice

The melting ice

That waters the future bed.

Then Spring will come

(Early for some)

With beautiful colors to see.

The cooling air -

Gentle breezes to share

Showing what life should be.

'Tis peaceful then

Where love has been

Called to share its beauty.

With herbs in time -

Rosemary and thyme -

We'll carry on our duty.

Soon Summer's storms,

And winds so warm,

The heat will oppress.

The rains come oft

From heaven's loft

Leaving a muddy mess.

The memories last

Of Summers past,

The scorching heat we knew.

Yet times we find

Comes to mind

Of gentle Summer dew's.

Now best of all

Still comes the Fall

Bringing Autumn's song.

The heavenly praise

Its voices raise

Singing so very strong.

With cooling breeze ,

And colorful trees

The Painter's brush did capture,

Showing to all

The beauty of Fall

Giving us spiritual rapture.

But soon it will end

With the cold, cold wind,

And snow covered mountains.

With the chilling air

Heavy coats we wear

To see the frozen fountains.

Of the seasons each year

Only Autumn brings tears

Of such joy to my eyes.

Yet its sad report

Is life is so short

Soon all living will die.

So listen, my friend,

To these words I send -

We all will give account

To the Father above

Who gave us His love

Sending Jesus to Calvary's mount.

He paid the cost

When He died for the lost

So death we needn't fear.

So walk with the Lord,

And reap heaven's reward

For death is ever near.

Now our Autumn's song

Can be so strong

If we live life so true.

To enter the gate

Would be so great

Where life's song is always new.

Then when Winter comes,

And the silence of drums

There will be no doubt

For Jesus will be

There to welcome thee,

You'll enter the gate with a shout.

When the spirit takes flight

To that land so bright

Born up on angel wings,

We'll then fully know

With faces aglow

The glory Autumn's song brings.

Gone Are the Days

Gone are the days of youth

When with vigor I sought truth;

Gone are the times of joy,

A time for laughter at my employ;

Gone are the times of fast pace,

When everything was like a race;

Gone are the years with the sorrows,

Now I look at so few tomorrows;

Gone are the tunes of sweet song

When I thought, I could do no wrong;

Gone is a life of youthful bliss,

Now comes the days the youth I miss.

One thing though will help me along -

Now I can sing the age-old song!

Tears in the Sand

Only God knows the tears I've cried.

He sees the hurts inside.

When I'm bent so low

It's to Him I go.

All those tears I've shed

While praying with eyes so red

Can be seen where I stand

For they are tears in the sand!

A Tender Heart

Do you have a tender heart

That at times is torn apart,

Or has your heart turned to stone

Since all you seek is your own?

Do you feel other's pain

As you greet them once again,

Or do you turn a blind eye

As you pass them walking by?

There's a Friend calling you

To show you love that's so true.

His name is Jesus Christ the Lord -

Eternal life is your reward.

When you answer to His call

He will keep you through it all.

A tender heart He'll give to you

So you can share with others too!

A Friend Indeed

The smile, the laughter, the pain, the tears

Have never faded through the years.

Even though we're miles apart

I still find you in my heart,

And miss your loving embrace -

The kindness and the grace.

Memories fill me day and night

Of how our friendship felt so right.

I long to see you again someday

As we walk along memory's way.

But until then all I need

Is to know that we are friends indeed!

A Special Friend

With eyes that shine

And hair so fine

She makes my heart to flutter!

So all day long

I'll sing the song

Of words my heart doth utter!

With such a smile

There is no guile

When my love for her doth show.

Such love for me

How can it be?

I really want to know.

She thrilled my heart

Right from the start

With a smile upon her face.

Now it seems

She'd fill my dreams

For in my heart she's found a place.

Now these words I send

To my special friend

A true gift from above,

One thing is true,

I'll tell it to,

She's filled my heart with love!

Don't Lose Hope

When in life's boat you're sailing,

The winds around are wailing,

And it seems you'll go under

Because of a silly blunder

Though you're frantically bailing,

There on the water One's walking,

And to you He is talking;

"My child I'm right here for you,

Trust in me I'll carry you through,

For Satan has come stalking.

I promised I'd never leave you.

To this promise I'm always true

Though rough the wind and rain

I'll carry you through all the pain

As I have done for others, too."

These words spoken we often quote -

"Remember He's in the boat."

The soothing words that He speaks

Will bring the peace that you seek -

The storms will pass as you will note.

Whatever you do don't let go the rope,

Facing problems He'll help you cope.

He's only just a prayer away,

He'll bring the peace come what may.

I charge you friend just don't lose hope!

A Broken Heart

When your heart is broken

Over words that were spoken

And it's tearing you apart

You've cried so many tears

Down through the years

From a broken heart.

You wander about

And fight off the doubt

That assails you inside.

But the pain you feel,

The hurt is real

And you simply can't hide.

Where do you go?

Whom do you know

That will show they care?

The heartache you see

Won't let you be

And it's hard for you to bear.

The only one

Is God's own Son

For He understands.

He tells you each day

That He is the way

So take Him by the hand.

When you feel blue

Here's what you do -

Just whisper a prayer.

Just call on His name

For He's always the same

And know that He'll be there!

At the Beach with God

When I'm feeling low

I'd really love to go

To the beach to be with God

As on the sand I trod.

The waves at the beach

He uses to teach

To trust in Him more

As we walk along the shore.

Though storm clouds may form

And I'm there in the storm

He's there to ever save

For He rides on the waves.

If I feel depressed

I have this one request

Lord take me to the beach

For there You will teach

That You ever will care

While hand in hand we share

Your loving heart You show

As in this walk we go!

Crossing Bridges

There are times in this life

Through the pain and the strife

We find bridges to cross

Due to a loss.

When the river is too wide

To reach the other side

We search every where

To get over there.

Those bridges that we find

That comes to our mind

Are ones we can share

With tender loving care.

Let's cross them together

Even in stormy weather

Though troubles down below

Seem only to grow

We'll cross those valleys wide

Unto the other side

And hold onto God's hand

For thus we will stand.

Crossing bridges we can learn

That some we need to burn.

Let's hold each other's hand

As we cross bridges again.

Dark Clouds

When dark clouds arise

And hide the starry skies,

Look for the silver lining.

It may seem no one cares

But God is still there,

His light is still shining.

When rain clouds appear

And fills you with fear,

Look for the rainbow.

Search for the day

He drives them away

To make you heart glow.

When it seems your boat

Will no longer float,

He's right there with you.

Just call on His name,

He's ever the same,

So know you'll make it through!

Family Together

There's nothing like family when you're down.

It always helps when they are around.

Through heartaches or sorrow keep them near,

For they'll bring you laughter, and cheer.

Where ever you go, bring them along

For they can help you to sing a bright song.

At the supper table when everyone's there,

Your heart will rejoice for you'll know they care.

Now listen my friends – what I tell you is true,

The family together is the best thing for you!

Faithfully Yours

What can I say, my love,

to show to you

that my heart is stable,

my heart is true?

How can I express, my love,

so that you will know,

to no other arms, I flee,

to none other do I go?

Where can I hide, my love,

such a love I give,

and such a life of love

that I now live?

Why would you question, my love,

the love I do not hide,

though others may not see

the story written inside?

When will you see, my love,

that this love is so real,

so real that time will not

change how I feel?

One thing is for sure, my love,

so certain is it tonight,

for no day or night could

keep me from the troth I plight.

Since I first saw you there,

my love, this is my plea.

I remain faithfully yours

and will always be.

Groaning Again

I'm groaning once again -

Crying deep within

For a soul that is lost

That doesn't count the cost.

They're walking on life's way

Blinded every day

By the cares of this life -

The troubles and the strife.

As they walk along

They're deaf to love's song.

Oh hear God's sweet voice

So that angels can rejoice.

Turn from the sin

And live once again!

Happy Is the Man

Happy is the man

That lives by God's plan.

The future he may not see,

But he's as happy as can be,

For he knows God holds tomorrow,

So from its pains he'll not borrow.

He follows everyday

Along the narrow way,

For God shines His Light

On the path that's right.

He trusts God's strong hand

To help him always stand.

The things that he has dreamed

Are fit for the redeemed,

For he dreams of heaven's land,

And someday he knows he'll stand

In the presence of God's Son

For the victory's already won.

Though he faces pain and sorrow,

And has no promise of tomorrow,

He is still pressing through

To live a life that is true,

To show others the way

To be happy every day.

He Knows My Hurt

He knows my tears

That I've shed through these years.

He knows my pain

That is like a stain

On my heart and mind.

The only peace I find

In all these years

I've shed these tears

Is to know God knows.

As the heartache grows.

At times it takes a toll on me

That others don't see.

Now this I'll ascertain

God knows I'm hurting.

Lord I Need a Hug Today

Lord I need a hug today,

Please send someone along my way

Who will hug like they love me,

Then I'll know it came from You!

The Feelings of the Heart

When you feel that your heart

Is torn all apart -

Those feelings inside

Are hard to hide.

Sometime they hurt so

You wish someone would know

How deep is the pain

As you feel it again.

When they look into your eyes

Do they see the tears you cry?

When all you really need

Is someone to heed

The groaning of your heart

That's been torn all apart.

I Have a Burden for You

I have a burden for you

And this is what I do -

I pray for you each day

That you will find the way.

This I must report

That the time is so short.

The signs are very clear -

The time of salvation is here -

So you must choose today

To walk the narrow way.

I tell you it is true

This burden I have for you

To share with you God's love

Born on wings of a dove.

The victory has been won

By Jesus, the only begotten Son,

So I'm making this appeal

With a burden that's so real.

What I say, I say to all,

Won't you heed that heavenly call?

Rising Above the Heartache

The things I have read

Have filled my head

With wonderful things.

Though heartaches may come

What I've learned from some

Is the joy it brings.

I know I can rise

To clear blue skies

Because of God's love.

Though heartaches may seem

To invade my dreams

I have a Friend from above.

He's promised to be

There always for me

To help me bear the pain.

When heartaches are near

He banishes the fear

And I rise up again!

The Path You Follow

What path do you follow in this life here below?

When the end comes do you know where you'll go?

There's a narrow path that leads up above -

Though at times it's rough, it's filled with God's love.

It started with Jesus as He hung on the cross,

For there He died to save the lost.

It continues to travel by an empty tomb

Where a risen Savior dispels the gloom.

It leads to heaven through the pearly gate -

To follow that path will only be great.

Another life's path is wide as can be

Where those that take can not be free.

It began at Eden where Adam and Eve

Due to their sin they had to leave.

Now we are born with sin our life

And we're bound to suffer much pain and strife.

If we keep following this destructive way

Then eternal death's sting will be our pay.

My friend I ask you what path you'll choose?

Choose the wrong one and your soul you'll lose.

I urge you to choose the path that's right -

For Heaven will be such glorious sight!

Scars of Love

What are these scars I see?

Are they there for me?

When You hung on the cross,

Was that because I was lost?

When they pierced You in the side,

A scar we cannot hide,

Was it to show us Your love?

What a gift from above.

Now they mean so much to me,

These scars of love that I see!

Your Calling

Do you know the calling on your life?

Can you answer amid pain and strife?

Have you made your calling sure?

In all the pressure can you endure?

Are you following in God's way?

Do you seek Him day by day?

When you are working on life's goal

Do you give thought about your soul?

No greater calling can there be

Than one that's answered on bent knee,

So spend some time what e'er you do

And hear God's voice – He's calling you!

Why?

Why do I feel I've a broken heart?

Why does it feel all broken apart?

Somehow the pieces seem so scattered,

And I really feel all torn and tattered.

Is there not someone who'll show they care?

Does somebody know that I need prayer?

Sometimes I cry until I groan,

And I'm living life so all alone.

Failed relationships are drowning me,

And I wonder if I'll ever be free.

The yoke I carry is full of pain -

When I look I see those tear stains.

So if you're passing by my way,

No matter the time – no matter the day,

Please lift me up and help me walk.

Just take some time so we can talk.

I need to know that you'll be there

To show to me you really care.

(Dedicated to all who are suffering today and

every day!)

Where Are The Tears?

Where are the tears for the broken hearts?

Can't you see they're torn apart?

Many are blinded and feel no pain

For those suffering a broken heart again.

Where are the warriors who'll fast and pray

For those in need of God's love each day?

Can't they see so many are lost?

Work now to save them at any cost!

Jesus is coming soon my friends

So let us endure unto the end.

Let the tears flow for those torn apart

So God can heal their broken hearts!

Living Your Dreams

Everyone should have dreams.

But so often it seems

We cast our dreams about

Because we are full of doubt.

We let our dreams fade

Living a life of facade.

We're bound by dreams of others

Whether family, sisters or brothers.

Failing to reach those dreams

Following others teaching it seems.

Overcome that fear now.

Take your dreams, somehow,

And turn them into you;

'Tis the only thing to do

To make your life to be true

If to no other than to you.

Live your dreams each day

As you walk along life's way.

You'll find each day brighter

And the load a little lighter.

Make Jesus your life-long dream

And on you He'll shine His beam.

He'll make your dreams come true

Because He really does love you!

Shackles and Chains

There were shackles and chains

And a heart full of pain

That were binding me so

No matter where I'd go.

I looked to the skies

With tears in my eyes,

And wondered how long

I'd sing my sad song.

Then Jesus came

And called me by name

To rescue me

And set me free.

He broke all the chains

And healed my pains.

He shows me each day

To live in the way

To follow our God

In the path I now trod.

No more shackles or chains

Will bind me again.

Though I look to the skies

With tears in my eyes,

They are tears of joy

Which none can destroy.

So my dear friend,

If you come to your end

Bound with shackles and chains

And a heart full of pain

Listen for His call

So your chains will fall.

I See You

I see You in the sunshine -

I see You in the rain.

I see You in my heartache -

I see You in my pain.

I know that You are with me -

Where ever I may go

I see Your hand of mercy

For this I love You so.

I see You in some faces

Of friends and love ones dear,

And know I'm not alone

For You are always near.

Though my life's journey

Will soon come to an end,

I know You'll be there

For You're my precious friend.

Though the path seems hard

One thing I know for sure -

With You walking with me

I know I shall endure.

You said You would lead me

On this heavenly way!

I'm longing now to see You

On that glorious day!

Relationships

Relationships are a work of art

To paint a picture of their lives

Bonding even when going through strives.

Relationships are lifelong endeavors

When dealing with all kinds of weather.

In order for each to learn to live

They must learn how to forgive.

66192697R00027

Made in the USA
Lexington, KY
06 August 2017